Contents

Flying by

Look! What is flying by?

It is a butterfly!

Little Creatures
Butterflies

raintree

a Capstone company — publishers for children

Raintree is an imprint of Capstone Global Library Limited, a company incorporated in England and Wales having its registered office at 264 Banbury Road, Oxford, OX2 7DY – Registered company number: 6695582

www.raintree.co.uk
myorders@raintree.co.uk

Editorial Credits
Carrie Braulick Sheely, editor; Juliette Peters, designer; Wanda Winch, media researcher; Tori Abraham, production specialist

ISBN 978-1-4747-2503-3 (hardback)
20 19 18 17 16
10 9 8 7 6 5 4 3 2 1
ISBN 978-1-4747-2507-1 (paperback)
21 20 19 18 17
10 9 8 7 6 5 4 3 2 1

British Library Cataloguing in Publication Data
A full catalogue record for this book is available from the British Library.

Acknowledgements
We would like to thank the following for permission to reproduce photographs:
Courtesy of Elaine Yim, 17; Dreamstime: Lukas Blazek, 21, psnoonan, 13; Shutterstock: aslysun, 19, 20, cipgysmo, 9, Doug Schnurr, 1, happykamil, 15, I love photo, back cover (butterfly), 3 (right), Kjersti Joergensen, 5, Lovely Bird, 3 (left), 24, Mau Homg, 14, Michael Shake, 7, OlegDoroshin, cover, Pan Xunbin, 6, Paul Reeves Photography, 11, pics five, note design, Tamara Kulikova, back cover, thanasit thinwongphet, 22

Printed in China.

A butterfly has four wings.
Soft, colourful scales cover
the wings.

scales

Brrrr! The air is cold.

A butterfly warms up

in the sun. Then it can fly.

Lunchtime

Two antennae search for food.

Does this flower have food?

Yes, it does!

antennae

11

Slurp! A butterfly drinks nectar through a long tube called a proboscis.

proboscis

Growing up

Tiny butterfly eggs hang from a leaf. A caterpillar will come out of each egg.

caterpillar

Chomp! It eats leaves.

It grows quickly.

Soon the caterpillar makes a case called a chrysalis. Inside the chrysalis, the caterpillar turns into a butterfly.

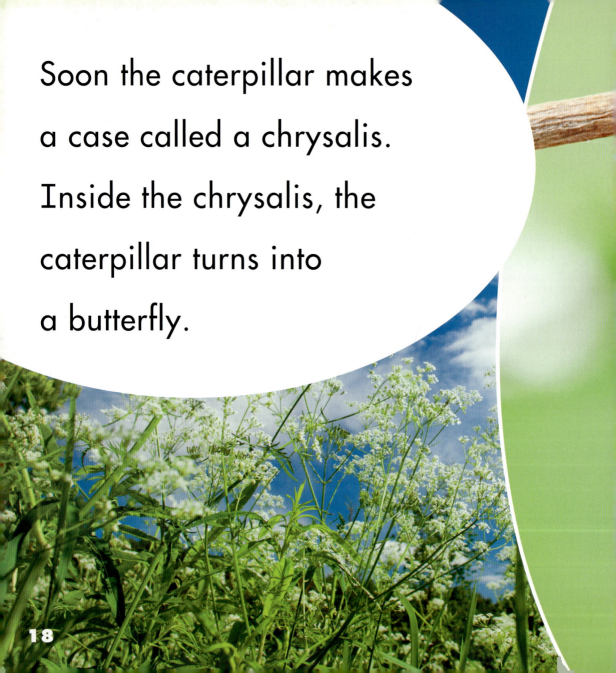

chrysalis

The new butterfly waits.

Its wings must dry.

Then it can fly away.

Goodbye!

Glossary

caterpillar larva that changes into a butterfly or moth; a caterpillar is the second stage of a butterfly's life cycle

chrysalis third stage of a butterfly's life cycle; pupa is another word for chrysalis

nectar sweet liquid found in many flowers

proboscis a long, tube-shaped mouthpart

scale small, thin plate that covers the wings of a butterfly

Read more

A Butterfly's Life (Watch it Grow), Nancy Dickmann (Raintree, 2011)

Caterpillars and Butterflies (Usborne Beginners), Stephanie Turnbull (Usborne Publishing, 2006)

Minibeast Food (Comparing Minibeasts), Charlotte Guillain (Raintree, 2012)

Websites

www.bbc.co.uk/cbeebies/shows/mini-beast-adventure-with-jess
Go on a minibeast adventure with Jess, and discover the minibeasts that are on your doorstep!

www.woodlandtrust.org.uk/ naturedetectives/ activities/2015/06/minibeast-mansion/
Design and build your own minibeast mansion!

Comprehension questions

1. Which body part do butterflies use to find food?
2. Why can't butterflies fly as soon as they come out of the chrysalis?

Index

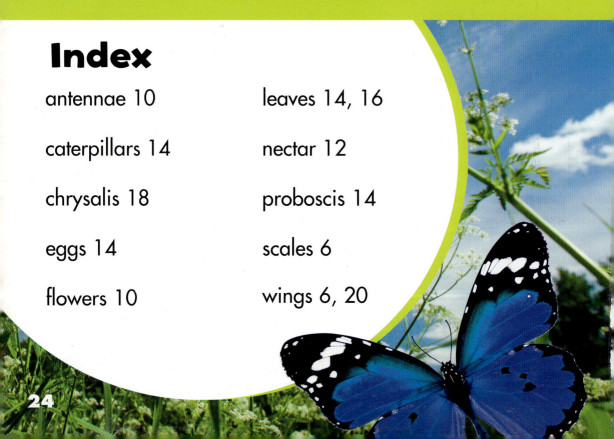